checked Sep·10, Dec·11.

Mental Activation

Mental Activation

Ways to stimulate your dog's brain and avoid boredom

Easy-to-do exercises that will make your dog

happy and well-behaved in two weeks

Anders Hallgren

Psychologist and animal behaviourist

CADMOS

Cadmos Verlag GmbH Brunsbek
© Copyright Anders Hallgren 2007
Title Photo: Prawitz
Design: Ravenstein + Partner, Verden
Typesetting: Nadine Hoenow
Print: LVDM, Linz

Printed in Austria

ISBN 978-3-86127-927-3

Contents

Mental Activation

Contents

No more boredom!

This book shows some simple exercises by means of which your dog can learn good behaviour in two weeks.

By attending to your dog's intellectual needs, mental activation provides a remedy for boredom, ensuring your dog is happy and contented.

Acknowledgements

My thanks to the Swedish behavioural research worker, Marie Hansson, who has raised mental activation to an art. Her bestseller, Min Bästa Vän ('My Best Friend') has inspired thousands of dog-trainers. Marie was one of my students in the early 1980s.

UNDERSTIMULATION

Why is mental activation so important?

Why is it so important to stimulate your dog's mind? So important that there is now a book about it? The foundation of this book's concept is based on a natural need in every canine, and if this need is not properly taken into account and dealt with, your dog will either become a problem dog or an unhappy dog—or both.

Dogs wait for people to start to play with them. Photo: Prawitz

Because dogs get bored!

Dogs do not activate themselves. They wait for their pack mates to take the initiative; if no one does, they become under-stimulated—not very unlike people!

Two studies that will surprise you

In the spring of 1977 I carried out some research on how active pet dogs are. In the wild, our dogs' natural relatives and ancestors, such as the wolf, spend many hours every day in motion. I expected to find that pet dogs would live up to their heritage as active animals, at least to some extent. I was also interested in finding out if too little exercise or mental activity, such as obedience and searching, could be related to problematic behaviour.

hours resting. Some 27% were active for four to six hours (at rest 18 to 20 hours). But most 39% rested for at least 20 hours.

The proportion of problematic behaviour was different for the three groups. In the active group, around half (47%) of the owners reported behaviour problems; most of them pointed out that these were minor problems.

Hours at rest	less than 18	18–20	more than 20
Distr. of dogs:	34 %	27 %	39 %
Problems:	47 %	75 %	82 %

Table 1: A study in a normal population of dogs, showing hours at rest and frequency of problematic behaviour.

Normal dog population

About 200 dog owners answered a questionnaire which asked them how much time their dogs spent moving around on a normal day, inside the house, in the garden or yard and on walks outdoors. Those who had any kind of problem with their dog's behaviour were asked to mention this, as well as how serious these problems were. The results are given in Table 1.

Almost 40% were inactive for 20 hours or more!

The table shows that one-third (34%) of the dogs in this study were active for at least six hours a day, in some way or another. That is to say, they were spending at most 18

Three-quarters of the dogs in the middle group had behaviour problems, and almost half of the dogs' owners pointed out that they considered the problems to be severe.

In the group with the passive dogs, the incidence of problem behaviour was larger still. A full 82% of the dog owners here reported problem behaviour, which a majority regarded as severe.

A population of problem dogs

In 1985 I made a further study, this time looking at problem dogs. In most cases I carried out a stress analysis, a tool I had developed that maps the amount of stress factors,

Hours at rest	Distr. of dogs:
less than 18	2.6 %
18–20	10.8 %
more than 20	86.5 %

Table 2: A study in a population of dogs with problematic behaviour, showing hours at rest.

among them under-stimulation. Some 342 stress analyses were done; the statistical results are shown in Table 2. The distribution in this group again revealed the importance of under-stimulation as a strong contributing factor behind problems in dogs.

Many dog-owners regard excessive digging as a disturbed behaviour. Photo: Prawitz

86.5% of the problem dogs were resting more than 20 hours per 24! Indeed, I discovered that 26.3% of the dogs rested 22 hours or more! Some problems, and not so very few, can be cured just by increasing the quantity of activity a dog gets in a day, as illustrated in the following case study. A veterinarian, who had examined her and found nothing medically wrong, referred an 18-month-old Dalmatian bitch. The symptoms were exaggerated scratching all over her body. The stress analysis revealed understimulation: she rested nearly 22 hour per 24. The advice was to activate the dog; after two days the scratching was as good as gone.

An experiment

In one small-scale experiment a dog was left alone in an enclosed field, with no one in sight. From a hidden observation place the frequency of his movements was registered for 20 minutes. At that point, another dog, known to him, was introduced for five minutes, and then that dog was taken out and the caretaker was introduced for five minutes. During the first 20 minutes the dog moved around three times, on each occasion for less than one minute, sniffing the ground. Most of the time the dog was sitting or lying down, with an empty expression in his face, waiting. When the other dog was introduced he made two initiatives to play and then become passive again. When his caretaker joined him for five minutes he made 13 initiatives to

Young puppies play extensively with each other, but later on often prefer a person as a playmate. Photo: Prawitz

move around, greeting, playing, exploring the field, marking etc. He was happy and active—not necessarily together with the caretaker, but to a great extent by himself, the caretaker being passive. This shows that dogs need us to be there for them to be active.

Literature on under-stimulation

As far as I know, there has been very little research on under-stimulation as a concept in dogs, although many writers have mentioned activity in wild canines (Mech, 1970; Zimen, 1981) and the need for activity and intellectual stimulation of dogs (Whitney, 1971; Fox, 1974; Trumler, 1984).

As Fox (1974) points out: *"...there may be few outlets or alternatives for many natural tendencies and basic instincts, so that they may be built up inside....What natural outlets does the pet dog have for hunting, tracking, stalking, biting, shaking and killing prey?....[N]atural tendencies might be controlled through punishment, but that would only bottle things up more."*

Fox also mentions that dogs "really need to work [and] ....break away from routine". Trumler (1984) states that *"the determining factor is that learning all these tricks, or work like that of working dogs, principally activates the brain."*

Whitney (1971) describes a dog in a kennel, trotting back and forth in his run, five hours every day, averaging 50 miles a day.

The conclusion is simple: the more a dog rests, the more surplus energy is built up, and this energy often finds expression in problem behaviour, in many forms and shapes. So the owner wishes that his dog would sleep more …

We have to realize that physical activity alone does not tire an individual as much as physical activity combined with mental activity does. Dogs that come home after an hour's walk with the owner are not very tired—sometimes quite the contrary. But a dog that has spent the same amount of time being trained in obedience, tracking, searching, or has been involved in any other mentally stimulating activity, normally is exhausted.

Balance between physical and mental energy

Many dogs are over-active; they display outbursts of energy and sometimes get out of hand. This energy may be due to different causes, but the two most common ones are too much and too intensive physical exercises, like running after balls, Frisbees or other dogs. Not that it is wrong to throw things for your dog to catch, but you must

not overdo it. The other is excessive energy stemming from resting too much and not getting enough physical and mental stimulation.

Looking at the dog's ancestors, wolves, we can learn much from the types of activities they engage in (Mech, 1970; Fox, 1975; Lopez, 1978; Hall and Sharp, 1978; Zimen, 1981; Peters, 1985). Our dogs are predisposed to occupy themselves with these or similar activities, and indeed often they have a real need for being physically and mentally active in the same ways.

Wolves and dogs are alike

Sharing many genes with the wolf, the dog is a very active animal, while at the same time being a pack animal, so it does not take many initiatives on its own. As a leader figure and a member of your dog's "pack"— the family—most of the initiatives must come from you. I can assure you that it will be a pure joy and a fulfilling and instructive experience to watch your dog mature, develop, and become harmonious and mentally satisfied. You may find how easy it can be to get your dog to stop barking, or stop doing other things that you find annoying. You will also be surprised by the new bond with your dog—a level of contact you perhaps never knew could develop.

In order to survive in an often tough environment and to get something to eat, a wolf has to cooperate with its pack members. They have to learn hunting techniques, follow trails, observe prey, outwit them, test them, follow them, chase them through rough and steep terrain, face them, attack them, avoid counter-attacks, keep in touch with their fellow pack members, and finally go for the kill. All these activities we have replaced with easy-to-chew, ready-mixed food served in a plastic bowl!

Behavioural synchronization

One may ask how it is that active animals like dogs can rest so much. The answer is

Dogs search out good vantage points in a house, from which to observe their owners and then wait for something interesting to happen. Photo: Lehari

simple, and can be formulated in two words: behavioural synchronization (Mortenson, 1975). Dogs are pack-living predators, and adult canines cannot engage in too many activities on their own. If they did, they would become tired, while the rest of the pack would be thoroughly rested after a good sleep. Then there would be an imbalance regarding the energy of the pack as a whole.

Pack animals must all rest at the same time and be active together, in order to be full of energy at the same time, for example before a hunt. The group is a powerful unit only if all its members are synchronized.

When wild canines leave "puppy hood" and mature, they become significantly more passive. Most activities are coordinated with the alpha wolves (Hall and Sharp, 1978), which ordinarily are the puppies' parents (e.g. Mech, 1970). When the leaders of the pack lie down to rest, so do the other members. When the leaders are active, so are the others. This coordination is a fact.

Our dogs are the same

Our dogs are so faithful to the heritage of their wild ancestors, that they still today, some 15,000 years later, function by their same rules of living. That is why your adult dog rests when you rest. And when you move about, the dog is following. This is why dogs follow their owner from one room to another, especially when they are fairly young.

Later they give up, because nothing comes of it. As the dog gets older, it learns that very little happens in the house, in spite of the owner's activities in different rooms. So the dog begins to place itself in strategic positions, usually in doorways, where it may observe more than one room at a time, carefully studying the humans as they walk around, looking to see if they go to the kitchen or to the front door.

Nothing wrong with my dog

Many dog owners think their dogs are good because they spend most of their time sleeping. Yes, they are good in the sense that they are not getting into any mischief. But what kind of life is this for a dog, sleeping it away? Dogs that do not get activated with walks and some mental tasks become bored. A bored dog is resting, awaiting some action to take place. And waiting, and waiting, and waiting....

While they are waiting, their body adapts to this low energy output; their metabolism turns down to a minimum and the whole hormonal system changes. The end product is a dog without initiative, sleeping the hours away, sleeping its life away.

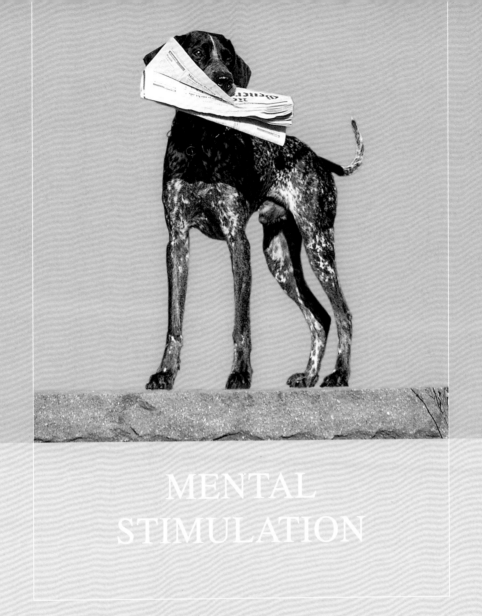

MENTAL STIMULATION

Give the dog some action

It is easy to understand why a dog can get bored. And it is likewise easy to see why a dog needs a little more attention, to have a full life and a couple of quality hours a day to fulfil its needs.

Fortunately for the dog owner who often may have problems with fitting things into the daily agenda, giving your dog this extra attention can be easy, funny and not very time-consuming at all. Many of the things you can do will be so easy and quick that you will be surprised. For example, putting out twenty small treats around the house for the dog to find, will take you only half a minute—but it may take the dog at least ten quality-filled minutes to find them!

Categories of activation

Looking at wolves, we find different activities which can be sorted under four categories.

1. Learning

Wolves learn a whole lot of things, from the time they open their eyes throughout their whole lives. They have to; otherwise, the existence of the individual, the pack or even the species, may be in danger. They learn a whole, complicated, language with many different signals; they learn submission and dominance in respect to members of the pack; they learn the behaviours of prey, and hunting techniques. Well, the list could go on for a few pages more, but this should give you the idea.

2. Solving problems

Food is not there ready and waiting in nature; prey animals have to be outwitted, captured and killed. This poses a whole lot of problems for the predator, because usually the prey animals are faster, and sometimes also heavier and stronger, then their predators. So wolves have to rely on intelligence more than physics, smartness more than muscle strength, and cooperation more than individual performance. As an example of their intelligence, I would like to tell you about a particular wolf pack in Canada. On their territory was an old closed-down power station, where many of the pylons were down, with lines hanging at different height above ground. This wolf pack used to find a moose pack, gently herd them towards the lines and, when they were close enough, concentrate on one victim and suddenly scare that moose to run into the lines, where it would get entangled and thereby become an easy prey.

3. Nose work

A wolf may follow the track of its prey animals for hours. It has to—or risks starvation. It has to put its nose against the wind and try to catch the tiniest smell of something to eat and it has to depend on its outstanding sense of smell to distinguish edible herbs and berries from those that could be poisonous. It communicates to some degree through this sense, for instance detecting which of its pack mates, if any, has left a mark of urine or faeces. And this is just a fraction of what wolves use their noses to accomplish. It is estimated that a dog's sense of smell is around one million times better than that of man's (Dröscher, 1969)! No wonder dogs can find hidden drugs, explosives and other things. Dogs have even been trained to detect tumours in people.

4. Balance

We usually walk our dogs on streets and easy trails, mostly because we prefer not to make too much of a physical effort ourselves. Anyone, though, who has watched an agility competition or seen hunting dogs run at full speed in the roughest terrain, will understand that dogs have inherited very

Agility training presents a physical and mental challenge. Photo: Lehari

good physical control. Most of the wolf's prey surely do not flee from their persecutors in easy terrain, they run uphill and downhill, climb hillsides and leap over holes and other difficult obstacles. A dog can run at high speed in rough terrain in the dark of the night, without stumbling. The portion of the brain of the dog that is devoted to physical control and balance, the cerebellum, is very well developed to enable this.

Mental stimulation solves problems

It is easy to see that dogs have not just the capability but also the need for mental challenges and experiences. If nothing happens in any day of a dog's life, it will be bored. This may very well be a cause for problem behaviour, not necessarily creating it, but surely making it more likely. This means that perfectly normal behaviour, like barking or jumping, may become so intense that you experience it as a problem. And to try to get rid of it by simply punishing the dog is not only nearly impossible, it is also unfair. To get the problem under control by mental activation is both effective and the right thing to do. You should aim to work with the cause, not the symptom.

Constantly punishing a dog for misbehaving will make it passive, submissive, and perhaps fearful of its owner, and may lead to a syndrome called "learned helplessness" (Seligman, 1975). This is to a great extent the same thing as depression, and Martin Seligman, a psychologist who has done extensive research on dogs, states that they are exceptionally susceptible to developing the learned helplessness syndrome.

Mental stimulation, on the other hand, will result in a happy and obedient dog, in a good relationship with its owner. It will also make you feel good; not frustrated by your dog's behaviour, but proud of it.

Since dogs must live their life on our terms, and in our homes, we cannot give them real mental stimulation of the type wolves get in their natural habitat, but we have to find activities that are as close as possible to the real experience. This is where human imagination and fantasy comes in. There are a lot of things that come close and are easy to do, that can put your dog's brain through the same gymnastics as the challenges wolves meet in the wilderness. Things that we can do outdoors or indoors, in the garden/backyard or in the kitchen, in the park or in the bedroom—really anywhere we choose.

You will see results from the very first day you start your dog on a mental activation programme. Your dog is going to be tired, satisfied and happy. Its willingness to cooperate will improve, and it will make more frequent contacts, care less for other people and dogs, be less intensive in other behaviours it normally indulges in, and it will also listen to you much more than before. There are no downsides or risks connected to mental activation—it is just giving the dog what it needs and wants, so that it can become the partner you really want it to be.

How much

For many dog owners, time is short, with long workdays, time spent travelling, shopping, cooking, cleaning, gardening, socializing with neighbours and friends, physical activities and—you name it. Where, in an already full agenda, could a dog fit in?

It is important for a dog to spend quality time with its owners, for example with retrieving exercises. Photo: Prawitz

Well, the heart of the matter is that if you have no time to devote to the basic needs of your dog, like for example daily walks, you should not be a dog-owner in the first place. To acquire a highly social, intelligent and dependent animal like a dog, and just leave it to itself, is wrong. A dog is a family member with needs very much the same as humans—we are not that different.

So if you are a caring person, you give the dog's basic needs a priority. If you cannot do it yourself, find someone that can take care of your dog during the hours you are away from home, someone that will walk it and give it attention and activate it, giving it the quality time it should have.

Usually, however, the question of finding time for the dog is easier than it seems at first glance. If you have a family, the time for dog activities can be divided between the family members. If the kids are too young or too small to walk the dog, they can work wonders with indoors activation—and they will enjoy it, because it is fun.

Have you ever felt that you need to get rid of some weight, but never come to a decision to start exercising? The dog will help you. Walking a dog for half an hour will burn around 250 calories. Walk the dog two times a day and you will burn 500 calories! And the dog's waistline too will start to get slimmer.

Most of the mental activities, as said earlier, will not take very much time, especially if you let the other family members in on them—and why shouldn't they, they are as responsible for the dog as your are. Of course some of the exercises are more time-consuming than others, but you can always choose the ones that fit best into your schedule for the moment.

How often

How often you should activate your dog is mostly a matter of your own possibilities. Good guidance is to be found in the activities of the wild wolf pack. For wolves, some days are filled with physical and mental activities, mostly in the form of hunting. But there are also "lazy" days when they rest most of the time, for example when they have killed a moose or a big deer, and the food is enough for a couple of days. Such times are spent not only in resting and sleeping, but also in playing.

I believe that, besides daily walks, some days could be more intensive for your dog than others, so if you feel one day that you have not devoted enough time to your dog,

do not let that be a burden of guilt. It is the same for natural-living canines and therefore not wrong for your dog. But it would be wrong to neglect the dog during weekdays and only activate it during weekends; that is too seldom.

This has special relevance to exercise. If a dog gets very little exercise for five days, and then a lot of walking, running and playing on Saturdays and Sundays, that could put too much effort and strain on the muscles, even resulting in permanent injury. Any athlete knows that muscles have to be worked daily, some days more, others less, and that a period of warming-up and stretching is necessary before any major effort. The same goes for dogs.

Balance between mental and physical activation

Experience has shown that a dog that gets roughly as much physical exercise as mental activation becomes the most harmonious. Of course there are individual and breed considerations here; for example, greyhounds seem to need more physical stimulus than mental. But it is a question of balance or quota, a relationship between the time spent in exercise and mental work.

As a rough guide, try to give your dog as much mental "gymnastics" as physical during an ordinary day. You will be able to see from your dog's behaviour when you have reached the best balance.

Hide-and-seek can mentally stimulate a dog. Photo: Prawitz

ACTIVATION TRAINING

The following are some suggestions as to what you can do, and how to do it, under the broad heading of mental activation, but they are certainly not intended to be a comprehensive list. A complete list would probably just restrict your imagination and keep you from coming up with tricks and other things of your own that may be especially useful for your dog. So look upon the following as suggestions only, and let your fantasy loose, finding out more mental challenges. Remember that there are almost no limits!

Always bear in mind that the actual learning of the different activities is the main thing here, not the performance of the already learned tricks. What is mentally challenging and tiring for the dog is working with its brain in trying to understand what to do—the learning process, not performing something it already knows. So if you should ever find yourself frustrated over slow progress on the part of the dog's comprehension or learning, think again. The longer it takes for the dog to grasp something, the more you may use a trick as an activation agent. If the dog learns something too quickly, you will end up having to find new tricks, and ultimately that could be a challenge for your imagination. Also, some of the activities are not suited for every dog, depending for example on the dog's size, so some of them you may have to forgo.

For every exercise, you will see described what it will look like when the process is completed and the dog knows what to do. You will also get a step-by-step process for training, and some suggestions on how to make it more difficult once it is completed. Besides that, you will find special observations, things to consider.

The activities to be intended to be achieved by getting the dog motivated to do them. There is no room for demands or force, something that would in any case be counter-productive. You have to get your dog motivated to do the things you want it to do with the help of toys, treats and an encouraging voice. You will find that this way is a superior way of training and that it enhances your dog's willingness to perform, and also deepens the understanding between you and your dog.

Learning

A dog can learn so very much. The limits are set more by your imagination than the dog's capability. Many of the things you teach your dog are really useful, some are just for fun.

The whole obedience programme that you can see in dog training classes, is a very good form of mental stimulation, at least during the process of learning. Since the ultimate goal of this book is not simply for you to get an obedient dog, but rather a harmonious one, it will focus on the first steps in obedience, not the perfection of performance.

Heeling
What it looks like:
The dog walks at your pace by your left side, looking up to you, seeking contact.

Step-by-step:
It is useless to try to teach any skill to a dog that is full of energy; first you have to walk the dog, and perhaps do some mental work before you start this exercise. Not until you see that the dog is reasonably calm, should you start.

Begin with the dog, off leash, sitting on your left. Show an attractive treat and hold this near your face, so the dog is encouraged to look up

At the beginning of the "heel" exercise the dog should remain on the left-hand side.

The dog should maintain eye contact while walking at heel. Photos: Lehari

at you. Any time it makes eye contact, say "Heel" in a happy tone of voice and start walking, all the time praising and repeating "Heel". Give the dog the treat after just a few steps and tell it that it is "Free". Turn your back to the dog and go away, so that "Free" does not mean something positive, but rather something negative, so it is eager to do the heeling again. After a short break, repeat the exercise, this time for a few seconds longer. Repeat no more than three times and then take a long break. Do this exercise no more than two or three times a day, successively for longer and longer, but never more than one minute—which is a long time for a dog to concentrate during the learning phase.

Make it more difficult:
Make turns to left and right and change speed.

Special observations:
Do not have the dog on its leash during the exercises, it should be sufficiently motivated by the treat. Watch your tone of voice when you say "Heel": you must sound glad and inspiring. At the beginning, train just for a few seconds—not longer—and do not train for more than one minute when the dog has learned to heel.

The usefulness of this exercise, besides the psychological stimulation, is that you can make the dog heel when you cross a street or pass children or other dogs or in a crowd. But do not let your dog do this for more than a short distance at a time.

The stand and stay exercise. Photo: Lehari

Stand and stand–stay
What it looks like:
The dog is standing on its four legs when you say "Stand", and stays when you leave and say "Stay".

Step-by-step:
Have the dog "stand", gently say "Stand", praise and give a treat. If the dog tries to sit, just entice it into standing up. If it blocks and

believes this is a sit exercise, you could put a hand on its belly while you entice with the treat. Do this no more than three times, then take a break and repeat later.

Before you advance to stand–stay, be sure the dog has comprehended the stand. Repeat it many times before you do the sit and down exercises, described later.

Make it more difficult:
Later, when the dog has learned these basics, you may train stand and stay longer and increase the distance more, but in small steps.

Special observations:
Be extra careful not to raise your voice in this exercise, because that could result in the dog sitting down.

Sit and sit–stay
What it looks like:
The dog sits when you say "Sit" and stays when you say "Stay" and take a couple of steps away.

Step-by-step:
Place yourself beside your dog, both facing the same way. Have your dog on your left side. Show a treat just above the dog's head, wait until it starts to sit and say "Sit" at that very moment, praise and give the treat. Then say "Free" in a neutral tone of voice, turn your back and take a break. Repeat several times, but let the dog sit for a few seconds longer each time, before it gets the treat.

When the sit is learned, have the dog sit at your left side and say "Stay" with a soft tone of voice, while you take a small step, just with one leg and praise gently. Return at once and give a treat. Repeat several times, but leave the dog a little bit further each time. Not further, though, than a few feet away. Mix the word "Stay" with praise: "Good, stay, good".

Make it more difficult:
Later, when the dog has learned these basics, you may train it to sit and stay longer and increase the distance more, but in small steps.

Special observations:
Do not advance the sit-stay too quickly. If the dog raises and comes to you, do not punish—instead, scold yourself for advancing to fast. A dog that makes mistakes and gets punished learns less well than a dog that makes it right every time.

The usefulness of this exercise, besides the psychological stimulation, is that you can have your dog sit and stay while you talk to a person or pick up broken glass etc.

Down and down–stay
What it looks like:
The dog quickly lies down, almost throwing itself to the ground, when you say "Down", and keeps that position when you say "Stay" and move a few steps away.

Step-by-step:
Have the dog off leash and ask it to sit. Reveal a treat, a little bit above its head, so

The sit and stay exercise. Photo: Lehari

During the down and stay exercise you can gradually move away from the dog. Photo: Prawitz

it looks up and is concentrated. Then with a quick movement lower your hand to the ground immediately in front of the dog. This should make the dog throw itself down to get the treat, and exactly as it lies down, gently say "Down". It is easier if you have the dog on your left side (see picture) during these first steps. Do this no more than three times, then take a break and repeat later.

When the down is learned, say "Stay" and stand up for one second, while gently praising, and repeat "Stay". Then give the treat while the dog is lying down. After a few repetitions, take one step away. Say "Stay" with a soft tone of voice, while you take the small step, praise gently and repeat "Stay". Return at once and give a treat. Repeat several times, but move a little bit further away from the dog each time. Not further, though, than a few feet away.

Make it more difficult:

Later, when the dog has learned these basics, you may train down and stay longer and increase the distance more, but in small steps.

Special observations:

Do not advance the down–stay too quickly. If the dog rises and comes to you, do not punish him, just go back and do it all over, but this time for a shorter time and distance.

The usefulness of this exercise, besides the psychological stimulation, is that you can have the dog in a relaxed position while you attend to some other things, but do not be away too long.

Walk ahead

What it looks like:

When you say "Ahead" (or whatever word you choose), the dog starts to walk in front of you until you say "Stop", "Heel", "Come" or "Free".

Step-by-step:

Always have the dog on a leash in this exercise. Every time your dog starts to go ahead of you, repeat the word "Ahead" and praise gently. After a few steps, say "Stop", stop it softly with the help of the leash and reward with a treat. Try to find narrow passages where you and the dog cannot go side by side and use them, preferably the same passages several times. This has to be repeated many times before it is learned. Only when you feel sure your dog knows what the word means should you try it in an open space.

Make it more difficult:

Get a longer leash or a rope and encourage the dog to walk further ahead of you, but not more than around ten feet.

Special observations:

You can never force a dog to walk in front of you. The slightest harshness of voice or attempt to push will be too forceful and will merely result in the dog coming to your side.

The usefulness of this exercise, besides the psychological stimulation, is that you can have the dog go ahead of you through passages or into a car, bus, train etc.

Walk behind

What it looks like:

When you say "Behind" (or whatever word you choose), the dog positions itself behind you as you walk along.

The pack leader walks in front; this exercise will strengthen the hierarchy in the pack. Photo: Lehari

Step-by-step:

Every time your dog happens to walk behind you, repeat "Behind" and praise. Motivate with a toy or a treat, which in the first sessions you hold behind your back, and give the reward after just a few short steps. Try to find narrow passages to use. When you think the dog knows the word, say it and praise when the dog walks behind. Later, do not have the toy or treat behind you to entice it, but give the reward at the moment the dog gets into the right position. After that you can wait for successively longer intervals before giving the reward. Remember to take frequent breaks.

Make it more difficult:

This is a challenge for your patience. Try to increase the distance between you and the dog walking behind you. Not too much,

This dog can crawl perfectly. Photo: Prawitz

though, just a couple of feet. You can accomplish this by selectively praising at times when your dog accidentally is a little bit further back from you.

Special observations:
The slightest harsh voice or trying to push will result in the dog coming up to your side. Keep the training time very short, especially at the beginning.

The usefulness of this exercise, besides the psychological stimulation, is that you can have the dog walking behind you through passages or into a car, bus, train, into a friend's house etc.

Crawl
What it looks like:
The dog moves a short distance in a lying position.

Step-by-step:

Ask your dog to lie down, show it a treat just in front of the nose and say "Crawl". Entice with the treat close to the dog's mouth, so it is easier for it to crawl an inch, rather than getting up and taking a step. Place one hand an inch above the shoulders of the dog, so if necessary you can prevent it from getting up. You may also use a bar, like a fence (see picture) or the like. Praise every small effort from the dog to crawl, with a gentle tone of voice, and give the treat immediately. Advance slowly, demanding an inch longer for each session. Do it just a couple of times per day.

Make it more difficult:

Ask the dog to crawl while you stand, or when you are a few feet away from him, successively increasing the distance.

Special observations:

This exercise put a lot of strain on to the joints, so be sure your dog has no hip dysphasia or anything of the like.

Come

What it looks like:

When you say, "Come", the dog runs up to you at full speed.

Step-by-step:

Practise this as often as possible, and always praise and reward intermittently with treats or toys. You can do this indoors as well as outdoors, in as many situations as possible which mean something positive for the dog: "Come" to get your food, "Come" to go for a walk, "Come" for a minute of activation, "Come" to get your treat, "Come" and let us play, etc. Also, let "Come" mean that you sometimes start to run from the dog as fast as you can, with its favorite toy in your hand. If you were to do this a hundred times a day, I dare to promise you near perfect results.

Making it more difficult:

There are many temptations in a dog's life: smells of all kinds, other dogs, children, people, birds, squirrels—you name it. Make a list of your dog's preferences, which things it is less likely to be interested in, and which it is most interested in. Start with those things that are easiest to get the dog to forsake to come to you on a recall, and advance to the more difficult ones. Teach it that after almost every recall it may go back to what had been so interesting.

Special observations:

Do not wait to praise until your dog has come up to you—that is too late. It is the coming that is to be reinforced, so praise all the way and give the treat or toy when the dog comes up to you.

To begin with, avoid saying "Come" if your dog is occupied by something very interesting, because that will teach it not to listen to your commands. Also, do not fall into the trap of becoming too controlling, guiding every step of the dog and making

The "Come here" command is important in all situations. Photo: Lehari

it submit its behaviour to your constant control. Give it the freedom to explore the surroundings, to read the "pee-mails" and other, more substantial, messages from other dogs and to experience the feeling of being an individual with its own rights—

and of course also obligations. "Come" is one of the most important obedience demands you can make of a dog, and its use is unlimited. In nearly all everyday situations, when it is off leash, this command will come in handy.

No

Most dogs never learn the word "No", in spite of the fact that it is one of the most common verbal signals used by us humans—sad to say. The reason is that the command is almost always given too late, when the dog already has started the forbidden act, by which time it is usually blocked and deaf.

If it is properly taught, you should not have to repeat "No" over and over again for the same offence.

What it looks like:

When you tell your dog "No", in a gentle but firm tone of voice, it immediately stops whatever it is doing. It just has to get away from there, but not necessarily go to you.

Step-by-step:

Here is what to do. You put a dish with some treats, not too attractive to begin with, on the ground. Walk with your dog on a leash towards it and say something like: "This is not for you, no", in a gentle tone of voice. When you are close to the dish, your dog will most probably block itself and go for the treats. In that second you take the grip, put your nose close to its nose and start to lay down the law. Gently say that these are forbidden treats and that you will not allow your beloved dog to ignore what you say, that next time you expect to be respected without having to raise your voice, and when you say "No" you really mean "No". The longer you keep this up, the more dominant you will appear to your dog .

After this, you start again, a few feet from the dish, and get close to it, reminding the dog that this is a No-No. If it does not obey, do it again. If it obeys, praise very much and give a treat from your hand. Repeat this exercise in a few different places so the dog will generalize and learn this lesson thoroughly.

Make it more difficult:

Place more attractive treats on the dish. Walk closer to it. Let the dog off its leash and pass it. Be further away from your dog when you say "No".

Special observations:

Do not shout "No": that is not necessary when you have taught the dog to obey a more soft-spoken "No". Nor should you use this word too often, as it could negatively influence the dog's initiative and make it submissive—or the dog could start to ignore it. Every dog must have a certain space in which to live, to do things, to investigate and to take initiatives on its own. If you are too much in control, the dog could lose its own feeling of control and become helpless (Seligman, 1975), as described earlier.

Being close, gripping each side of the dog's neck, is a very sensitive situation and you could become too dominant if you do this harshly, especially if you raise your voice. Done right, it should not seem hostile or unloving. Also remember that this method may not work with every dog, although it does with most. So if it does not work with

Only when the dog establishes eye contact is he allowed to fetch the toy or treat. Photo: Prawitz

yours, find something else to teach "No", like a spray of water on the nose.

Eye contact

What it looks like:

The dog makes eye contact with you, awaiting your instruction as to what he must do.

Step-by-step:

Allow your dog to watch, as you throw a toy or treat. He should not be allowed to jump after it, but should stay sitting quietly beside you. Wait patiently. Sometimes you will have to wait a long time, but as soon as the dog looks you in the eyes, let it then fetch the toy or treat.

Initially, make no effort to attract your dog's attention. If it doesn't work, however, and your dog spends the whole time gazing after the toy or treat, then try to attract its attention by making a noise. You can move slightly closer to your dog. Keep your attention fixed on it.

Make it more difficult:
Gradually extend the distance between yourself and the dog.

Special observations:
Sometimes, eye contact can be very fleeting, so you must remain very attentive.

Dress
What it looks like:
When you hold the collar in front of the dog, it puts its head in it.

Step-by-step:
Hold the collar—preferably a leather collar, so it is wide enough—in one hand, just in front of the dog's nose, and a treat in the other hand at the other side, enticing it to take the treat through the collar. Repeat, but do not forget to take breaks. When the dog seems to know what you mean, do it without treats, but instead with a walk as a reward. Hold up the collar and do not open the front door until your dog is dressed.

Make it more difficult:
If you have a chain collar, this will be more difficult for the dog to get into. You could

also let the dog jump up on you (if that is permitted), or stand up by itself or with the help of a chair (see picture). You can also lower the collar so the dog almost has to crawl.

Special observations:
If the dog has a joint problem, it should not be made to jump, stand up on its hind legs or crawl.

Get the newspaper
What it looks like:
When you tell the dog to "Get the newspaper" it rushes out and (assuming the newspaper boy is in the habit of leaving the newspaper somewhere on your property, perhaps at the garden gate or wherever) gets it for you, no matter if it rains or shines.

Step-by-step:
To train this with treats may be a little bit risky, because dogs usually drool when they anticipate something to eat, which could spoil the paper. But if you praise enough and go slowly to the jar where the treats are, you probably will circumvent this problem.

You also have to take another risk, namely that it could tear the paper, but this is just through the first trials, before the learning is established. To begin with, use old papers.

Roll a newspaper and secure it with a piece of string so it will not unfold. Use it as you would use a stick to play with, but

Retrievers enjoy fetching the newspaper. Photo: Lehari

do it indoors. Tease the dog a short while, so it becomes interested and wants to catch the paper, then throw it and encourage the dog to get it. Exchange the paper for a treat. Repeat a couple of times and then take a break. Repeat again after a while. Use a new paper, so the dog does not believe that it is just this one to play with.

When you have got the dog enthusiastic with this play, stop throwing the paper and instead just show it and hide it, gradually closer to the usual point of delivery, and let the dog find it and bring it to you in exchange for a treat. But from now on, while praising, you extend the interval slightly before the dog gets the treats.

The next step is to put a training paper at the same place where you usually find your morning paper. The dog is to wait inside. Allow gradually longer intervals between placing the paper and sending the dog. When you find that the dog does not dribble on the paper or tear it, you are ready to let it get your real morning newspaper.

Make it more difficult:
Sometimes the papers come in a plastic bag, so repeat the process with such, but just a few times will be necessary.

Special observations:
Your neighbours will be envious.

Lick your mouth
What it looks like:
When you say, "Lick your mouth", your dog puts out its tongue and licks from one corner of its mouth to the other. Guests at the dinner table usually are very impressed with this.

Step-by-step:
Have your dog sit, and show a treat. Move your hand from a few inches to the dog's nose and back again, repeating "Lick your mouth". In the very instant you see the tip of the tongue, praise and give the treat. Do this a few times and take a break. To advance, wait until you see more and more of the tongue before you reward.

Make it more difficult:
Increase the distance gradually between yourself and the dog.

Special observations:
This is quickly learned by the dog, I am sorry to say, but during the actual learning phase it is good mental gymnastics.

Dead dog
What it looks like:
When you say "Dead" or "Bang", your dog lies down on its side.

Step-by-step:
Ask the dog to lie down and encourage it to roll over to one side with the help of a treat. Probably this will take some time for the dog

Dogs learn quickly to lick their noses. Photo: Prawitz

The dog should be completely relaxed during this exercise. Photo: Prawitz

to understand—which is good. Repeat "Dead dog" or "Bang", and praise when it obeys.

Make it more difficult:
Let your dog be "dead" a little bit longer before it "comes to life" again.

Special observations:
Avoid forcing it with your hands, because that will only make the dog resist.

Roll over
What it looks like:
The dog rolls over on its back when you say "Roll over."

Step-by-step:
The best starting point is from Dead dog, when your dog lies on the side. Hold a treat near its nose and move your hand towards the dog's ribs. Say a gentle "No" if it tries

to stand up. The dog will follow with its head (see picture) and also with its body position. When it moves its body just slightly, praise and give the treat. Repeat — with breaks interspersed — but demand a little more change of body position every time, so it looks more and more like a roll over, and finally is.

Make it more difficult:
Get your dog to roll over several times, and to stay on its back in the middle of a roll.

Special observations:
Do the exercises on a flat and soft ground, so nothing hurts the dog when it rolls. The vertebrae are sensitive to pain.

It is better to practise rolling on soft ground. Photo: Prawitz

Kissing is actually a soothing gesture. Photo: Prawitz

Kiss

What it looks like:

When you ask for a kiss, the dog licks your mouth or chin.

Step-by-step:

Since dogs will lick people's faces out of pure joy, this normally comes naturally. Whenever your dog licks you, just say "Give me a kiss", and praise. If repeated a sufficient number of times, the word "Kiss" gets the dog conditioned to licking your mouth.

Make it more difficult:

Get the dog to kiss you on the cheek, by specially rewarding it when it accidentally licks beside your mouth. This places a demand on you to have quick reflexes and reinforce at the very second the dog licks your cheek.

Special observations:

Not everyone likes to be "kissed" by a dog. If you do not like it, there are many other activities to indulge in..

Point at mouth and nose

What it looks like:

When you ask the dog to point at your nose, mouth or ear, by asking it, "Where is my nose?", or "Where is my mouth?" etc., it points at the right one with its nose.

Step-by-step:

The easiest way to teach this exercise is to go from the kiss to the pointing. Instead of just praising the dog for kissing, you reward it with a treat. Since most dogs are in a hurry to get the reward, it will hasten to give you a kiss, sooner or later with just the tip of the tongue. Soon it will be just a quick point with the nose.

When this is established, reward the dog when it accidentally touches your nose.

Make it more difficult:

When the dog knows how to point at your mouth and nose, you ask it to point at your ear. Repeat the words "Where is my ear?", and let the dog find out what you mean, but give a little help by turning your head. If you hold back the reward when the dog touches your nose and mouth to get its treat, it starts to point at other places to. When it comes to the cheek, a little bit closer to your ear, praise and reward.

Special observations:

If the dog becomes frustrated and has obvious difficulties to understand what you mean, especially when it comes to pointing at your ear, give some help by holding a treat close to your ear, or put a drop of gravy or sauce on your ear lobe.

Whisper

What it looks like:

When you say in a suitably hushed tone of voice, "Whisper", the dog puts its nose to your ear for a few seconds.

When a dog invites you to play like this one, you can teach it to bow as well. Photo: Prawitz

Step-by-step:

The easiest way to teach this is to put a drop of gravy or sauce on your ear lobe as for the first trials. When your dog has conditioned the command "Whisper" to that, you hold a treat in your hand, without the dog knowing it. When it touches your ear, to look for the gravy, praise and reward instantly.

Make it more difficult:

Teach the dog to whisper for a longer time.

Special observations:

Be prepared to go back to earlier stages in this exercise, by putting some gravy on your ear lobe, if the dog seems to become confused.

Bow
What it looks like:
The dog bows its head when you command "Bow" or "Say hello".

Step-by-step:
In this exercise you have to wait for the dog to look down at the floor. Hold a treat in your hand and wait for the dog to look down the slightest bit. Praise and reward instantly. Just keep on and selectively reward deeper "bows", and the dog will learn this.

Make it more difficult:
Have the dog do a really deep bow, by selectively rewarding only the deeper bows and holding the bow position gradually longer.

Special observations:
You may have to be very patient to get the dog to stop trying to hypnotize the hand that is holding the treat, so do not give up too easily.

Look left–look right
What it looks like:
When you say "Look left" or "Look right", the dog turns its head in the correct direction.

Step-by-step:
In this exercise you have to wait for the dog to look away from you in the direction you say, as seen from the dog's position. Hold a treat in your hand and wait for the dog to look left the slightest bit. Throw something so as to make a noise on the dog's left side. Praise and reward the instant it turns it head. Repeat several times, with frequent breaks in between and with lesser and lesser help by making the noise. Alternate between left and right.

Make it more difficult:
Have the dog hold its head in the left or right position for a second and praise, by gradually delaying the treat.

Special observations:
You may have to be very patient to get the dog to stop trying to hypnotize the hand that is holding the treat.

Left paw–right paw
What it looks like:
When you say "Left paw" or "Right paw", your dog gives you the correct one.

Step-by-step:
To lift a forepaw comes naturally to dogs, since it is a signal that is prioritized in their communication repertoire. However, should you experience difficulty in getting your dog to raise one of its forepaws, you can hold a treat in your clenched hand, keeping that low in front of the dog. This will encourage it to open your hand by scratching. Immediately it does that, open your hand and give the reward. After the dog has learned that, let it scratch your hand but give the treat from the other one. Also slowly raise your hand more and more up from the low position. Your dog

The most difficult part of this exercise is to distinguish left from right. Photos: Prawitz

will probably change paws by itself on and off in this exercise. So whatever paw it uses, you say the word for that paw, "left" or "right", as seen from the dog's position. After enough training it will start to condition one word to each paw, although you probably will have to do some gentle corrections.

Make it more difficult:
Teach the dog to raise the paw higher by selective reward.

Special observations:
Some dogs have elbow disorders that can make lifting a forepaw too high painful. Be sure your dog is free from any such disorders.

Give me five
What it looks like:
When you say, "Give me five" and hold up the palm of your hand in front of your dog, it puts up its paw and meets it.

Step-by-step:
This is in a way a development of the previous exercise, but you work with just one of the dog's paws, preferably the right. Begin with teaching the dog to scratch your right hand to get the treat you hold in it, and gradually raise it. When your dog lifts its leg high, have your hand open, holding the treat with just your thumb. Next step, have the treat in your other hand and praise and give the treat instantly when the dog touches your hand with its paw.

Make it more difficult:
Let the dog come up to you from a distance and "give you five". Let the dog stand on its hind legs and "give you five".

Special observations:
Some dogs have elbow disorders that can make lifting a forepaw too high painful. Be sure your dog is free from any such disorders.

Wave
What it looks like:
When you say "Wave", or something like it, your dog waves its right paw at you.

Step-by-step:
This is quite like the previous exercises, but the dog moves its paw so it looks like waving. Let the dog scratch your hand to get the treat, keeping it low at the start. Every time the dog tries to scratch your hand, move it so it scratches in the air, praise and reward. Then let it scratch without touching your hand successively more times before rewarding. Also raise your hand a little bit as the "waving" develops.

Make it more difficult:
Have the dog wave for a longer time. Ask it to wave from a distance.

Special observations:
Some dogs have elbow disorders that can make lifting a forepaw too high painful. Be sure your dog is free from any such disorders.

Waving from a distance. Photo: Prawitz

Push buttons

What it looks like:

When you say "Push the button" or "Ring the bell", the dog puts its nose or paw on the button. Only for bigger dogs.

Step-by-step:

Decide if you want the dog to use its nose or its paw. The nose is more difficult, but with the paw the dog may leave a mark on the wall. Hold your hand with a treat close to the door bell, enticing your dog to put its nose to your hand or scratch it with its paw, whatever you have decided. Praise and reward. After a few repetitions, selectively reward when the dog, probably accidentally, puts its nose or its paw beside your hand, closer to the button. Go on from there and reward profusely when it hits the button, no matter whether it pushes the button or not.

Next time, praise more moderately, but do not reward with treats, when your dog touches the button. This will make it a little bit frustrated and it will push harder. The instant that happens, reward with several treats and praise highly.

Make it more difficult:

Teach the dog to ring the doorbell when it is alone outside and wants to come in.

Special observations:

If the dog has any joint problems it should not be made to jump or stand up on its hind legs.

Ashamed

What it looks like:

When you ask, "Are you ashamed?", the dog puts a forepaw over its face.

Step-by-step:

This is rather like the former exercises, but in this you combine leg lifting with having the dog lower its head. Start by sitting opposite the dog with a treat in your hand, kept a little bit over your dog's head, but a little to the side, and encourage it to scratch the hand. This will make the dog lift its paw above its head and move the leg a little bit more sideways. When it does, praise and reward. Having learned this, wait until it puts up its paw closer to its face before you reward. Try to give the treat from under the paw. Then use discriminatory reward as the paw comes closer to the face.

Should the dog accidentally put its paw close to, or even touch its face, as dogs may do to scratch or remove something from their faces, say the word and praise profusely, and give extra treats. Otherwise work towards having the dog lower its head a little and putting the paw more and more close to the face. Finally let it hold the "ashamed" position for successively longer time.

Make it more difficult:

This is already difficult enough.

Special observations:

This is a time-consuming exercise that will put a big load on your patience as a dog

The "be ashamed" exercise is difficult and requires a lot of patience. Photo: Prawitz

trainer. There are other ways to train this, for example with the training method called "shaping", but we do not want it to be too easy, because the goal is not the performance of the dog, rather it is to get the dog to work with its brain.

Also, please observe that, as far as we know, dogs do not feel shame. What you see when the dog looks ashamed—perhaps for chewing up your favourite slippers—is just body language for submission, intended to inhibit aggression.

Zigzag
What it looks like:
As you walk forward, the dog zigzags between your legs.

Step-by-step:
Start with your dog sitting at your left side. Put your left leg forward and entice the dog with a treat, held between your knees (see picture), to go through the "tunnel", as you say "Zigzag". Then put your right leg forward and entice the dog to go through again, this time from your right side. When you have done this so many times that you can see that the dog feels comfortable with doing this, gradually walk faster, but do not advance too fast.

Make it more difficult:
Walk longer distances. Walk with smaller steps. Stand still and let the dog do "figures of eight" between your legs.

Use a treat to tempt the dog to walk between your legs.
Photo: Prawitz

Once the dog has learned this exercise, it can walk around you in a figure of eight. Photo: Prawitz

Special observations:

Many dogs feel uncomfortable going between a person's legs, and hesitate in the beginning. Do not push or pull, it will just make the dog hesitate more.

Jump through

What it looks like:

You hold your arms in a ring and say "Jump through", and the dog jumps through your arms. You can also use a plastic ring.

Step-by-step:

Use an attractive toy or a stick and place it on the ground in front of you. Let the dog sit by your side, form a big circle with your arms and hold them near to the ground. Do not close the ring as that would create too small an opening, but hold the opening a little bit sideways, so the dog does not just walk through. Hold your arms close to the dog and tell it to jump through in an encouraging tone of voice, and praise it when it does.

Next, gradually close the ring and raise your arms up from the ground until the dog jumps high and through a smaller circle, with your hands together.

Make it more difficult:

Teach the dog to jump through all kinds of rings you can find. There are dogs that have learned to jump through burning rings, but I would not encourage you to teach that!

Special observations:

Do not look at the dog when it starts to jump, it could collide with your head, become scared and cause you an injury. Always turn your head away.

Jump over legs and arms

What it looks like:

You hold out a leg or an arm and the dog jumps over it when you say "Jump!"

Step-by-step:

Entice your dog with a stick, toy or treat to jump over your leg, stretched out and held as low as you can, your foot touching a tree or a wall. Keep the dog on leash so as to keep it from going around you. Encourage it to jump and praise when it does, even if it only takes a small step over.

Make it more difficult:

When the dog has comprehended the jump over a leg, do the same thing with an arm, but this is much more difficult, so be patient and reinforce more.

Special observations:

Dogs with hip dysphasia and other joint problems should be prevented from jumping too much.

Fetch

What it looks like:

When you point at an object or say the name of it, the dog brings it to you.

You can practise this with small dogs in the house.

As an alternative you can let the dog walk underneath your legs. Photos: Prawitz

Step-by-step:
There are several ways to teach a dog to retrieve. The easiest and most common way is to play and throw a toy or a stick and reward when the dog gives it back.

Tease your dog with a toy and, when it is ready to run after it, throw the toy, but not too far, saying, "Fetch!" Praise when it takes the toy, and ask it to come. Exchange the object for a treat. Repeat a few times and then take a break. Repeat this exercise, but with different attractive objects. Reward with treats because that will get the dog more focused. Only give the reward when the dog places the object in your hand, not when it drops it at your feet.

Make it more difficult:
Teach the dog to retrieve things that it usually would not take in its mouth, like keys.

Special observations:
Running after sticks and balls too much may cause the dog to be over-stimulated and may lead to stress, so do not overdo this and do not throw very far. Do not use this kind of play as a way to give the dog its physical exercise.

Clean up
What it looks like:
The dog picks up things like pieces of paper from the floor and puts them in a wastepaper basket when you say "Clean up".

Step-by-step:
This is the same as fetch, but instead of retrieving the object to you, the dog puts it

Special dog toys or dummies are ideal for retrieving exercises.
Photo: Prawitz

When tidying up, the dog collects its toys and places them in a special container. Photos: Prawitz

in a waste-paper basket. Place one of the objects the dog retrieved before on the floor. Hold your hand over a low waste-paper basket, and when your dog is to give you the object, remove the hand so the object falls into the basket. Praise and reward with a treat. Repeat several times, but with different objects, and gradually removing your hand from the waste-paper basket.

When you train mental activation indoors, one very good exercise is for the dog to tear open paper boxes (see page 71). So there will be pieces of paper on the floor now and then. For this reason it is a good thing to have previously taught the dog to put these in the basket. But begin with larger pieces of paper. Take a sheet of paper, squeeze it into a ball and tease the dog with it. When it seems eager to take it, throw the paper ball on the floor and say "Clean up!", and reward the dog for putting it into the basket.

Make it more difficult:
The smaller the piece of paper the dog is told to "clean up", the more difficult it is. Cleaning up when the waste-paper basket is in another part of the room than where you stand is also more difficult.

Special observations:
None.

Roll the ball
What it looks like:
Your dog puts its nose to the ball and pushes it to you.

Step-by-step:
Your dog has to really know "down and stay", because in this exercise it will be lying down through the entire process. Hold a very attractive treat in your hand, put a ball between the front legs of your dog and repeat "Roll the ball" or "Push the ball." Praise every time it looks at the ball or even looks down. Should your dog touch the ball the slightest, even if it does not roll, give a small piece of the treat and wait for the dog to do it again. Let it find out for itself what it is supposed to do to get the reward, and soon it will roll the ball in your direction, pushing it with its nose.

Make it more difficult:
Place yourself at a greater distance from your dog, or at another angle.

Special observations:
No special observations other than that you must be patient.

Talk
What it looks like:
The dog barks and growls in different intensities when you ask it to "Bark", "Speak", "Murmur", and the like.

Step-by-step:
Most dogs bark easily — some way too easily — so the behaviour is already established, but it is conditioned to different cues, like the doorbell etc. Usually you do

not want to reinforce such barking. So we have to find something else that will get your dog to bark. The best thing is to tempt it with a toy. You play with the toy and let the dog watch. When it gets sufficiently excited and frustrated because it cannot have the toy, there most probably will be a bark. At that moment, say "Bark" or "Speak", or whatever you have chosen, and give the toy to the dog.

Sometimes it could be advantageous to have the dog on a leash or behind a fence to get it sufficiently upset, so as to release a bark. An alternative is to have it behind a door, hearing you playing with its toy. The frustration could make it bark, and if so, you immediately open the door and give the toy as a reward, repeating the word a few extra times.

Once you have got the bark conditioned to the word, you start with a less intensive sound, like a quieter bark. This is easy, because in a situation where you just hold the toy and do not play with it, the dog is less upset and therefore the bark will not be as strong.

Several times your dog will growl as the first attempt to bark on command. In these cases you quickly change the word to "Murmur", or whatever you have chosen. After that, all you have to do is continue with these exercises and put the finishing touch to them.

Make it more difficult:
Move to conditioned other sounds, like whimper or whine.

Barking on command should not be connected with aggressive behaviour. Photo: Prawitz

To teach a dog to shake on command takes a lot of time. Foto: Prawitz

Special observations:

Sometimes people are tempted to condition the word to barking when the dog barks aggressively at another dog or at a stranger at the door. However this could simply serve to reinforce the aggression and is therefore not advisable.

Shake

What it looks like:

When you say, "Shake", your dog shakes like when he is wet.

Step-by-step:

This behaviour is already established in the

Especially in unfamiliar surroundings, it can be useful if the dog learns to pee or go to the toilet on command. Foto: Lehari

behavioural repertoire, and it is easy to predict its occurrence. So when the dog is wet and you see that it is starting to shake, just repeat the word several times and praise in between. This will take some time to condition, so you will not see any progress for a while, depending on how often the dog gets wet.

Go pee, go potty
What it looks like:
The dog pees or poops only when you tell it to.

Step-by-step:
This behaviour, like shaking, is already well established in the behavioural repertoire and

it is quite easy to predict its occurrence. So when the dog is starting to pee, just repeat the word "Pee" (or whatever you choose) several times, and praise in between. Do the same when the dog starts to poop, but with the relevant word for that. This will take some time to condition, so you will not see any progress for a while.

Special observations:
Do not use this unless there is some need on the dog's side to unload.

Yawn
What it looks like:
The dog yawns when you tell it to.

Step-by-step:
This behaviour is also already well established in the dog's behavioural repertoire, and it is quite easy to predict its occurrence. So when the dog is starting to yawn, just repeat the word "Yawn" (or whatever you choose) several times, and praise in between. This will take some time to condition, so you will not see any progress for a while.

Stretch
What it looks like:
The dog stretches when you tell it to.

Step-by-step:
This behaviour, like the previous one, is already well established in the behavioural repertoire and it is easy to predict its occurrence, which is when the dog wakens after

a sleep or is getting ready for a walk. So when it starts to stretch, just repeat the word "Stretch" (or whatever you choose) several times, and praise in between. This will take some time to condition, so you will not see any progress for a while.

There certainly are more things to find out to teach a dog than are presented here, so use your imagination, listen for tips from others and include new tricks in your dog's agenda.

Solving problems

Dogs are intelligent animals and so are their ancestors, the wolves. They have to be intelligent in order to survive. Among other things, they have to use their brains in solving all the problems that they meet in trying to get something to eat. Just as an example, I would like to mention one thing you do not find in every animal species, the ability to figure out angles. When a prey animal flees, wolves are able to take a short cut and overtake it, calculating the speed and the direction of the prey and anticipating where they will intercept.

Dogs also have this ability. If you roll a ball from an angle at a wall, the dog anticipates where to meet the ball before it bounces back, and will catch it at that very point. Creating problems for your dog to solve is really a good form of mental activation, because it really has to use its brain power and it is a very natural kind of activity. So here follow some suggestions, but do try to find other problems to present to your dog by using your imagination.

Detour

What it looks like:

You are for example on the other side of a fence and ask the dog to come. It has to make a detour, leaving you and looking for the gate, to be able to get to you. You can also make the dog take a detour to get a toy or a treat that you have thrown on the other side of a fence.

Step-by-step:

Place your dog in a fenced area. Throw a ball or a stick for the dog to retrieve and then leave through the gate without the dog observing you. Depending on how insecure you think it is going to be at seeing you at the other side, walk away to a distance where it will be motivated to get to you, but not too anxious.

It is a mental challenge for the dog to work out an alternative route in order to reach its goal. Photo: Lehari

Call the dog and encourage it to come. Just wait and let it solve the problem by itself. If it seems to be too anxious, move closer to the gate. If it does not make any effort to come, walk away, hide behind something and call again.

A detour problem may be set in the house if you have a room with two doors, both leading to the same room. Leave the dog in the room, close the door but leave the other open. Stay outside by the closed door and ask the dog to come to you. Then it has to leave the door where you are and go through the other one to get to you.

You may create a good detour problem just by throwing a toy or a treat on the other side of a fence or a wall, and letting the dog find its way in.

When you are out walking your dog on the leash, there will be many times when you end up on either side of a tree or a pole. Most dog owners will walk back and go the dog's way, or pass the leash around the pole. Do not do that. If your dog walks on the wrong side of a pole (see picture) there will be a problem, and you are not the one that caused it. Your dog did, so it is up to him to find the solution. Just call and wait until the problem is solved. To make it a little bit easier in the beginning, you could hold the leash as short as possible.

Make it more difficult:
Go to the opposite end of the fenced area and call your dog. If you have presented it with a detour problem inside the house, you could walk out of the house and around, up to a closed door or window and call. On the wrong side of a pole, give the dog a long leash, so it has to walk away from you longer, to go around the pole.

Special observations:
If the dog gets anxious at any time, this may block its ability to work out the right way and it will then panic, so get closer immediately.

Disentangle leash from legs
What it looks like:
The dog has turned and got the leash under its leg, and stands looking at you with a silly smile. You say, "Lift your leg", or something like that, and the dog lifts its leg and gets the leash right.

Step-by-step:
Do not use treats in this exercise, because that could get the dog focused on the treat instead of trying to get the leash off from its leg. Put the leash under the dog's front leg, but let it hang loose in a bow, touching the leg down by the foot (see picture). Encourage it to lift its leg, saying, "Lift your leg", at the same time you tighten the leash a little bit, so it touches the foot somewhat harder. Praise immediately when the dog lift its leg, even if it does not succeed in disentangling the leash. Do it just a couple of times per walk. Anoth-

A dog should be able to free itself from such a trapped position. Photo: Lehari

er way, sometimes simpler, is to stop the moment the leash gets entangled, hold it tight, though not so tight that the dog must lift its leg too high in order to get it right. Do not take another step until the dog disentangles. When it does, praise and walk on.

Make it more difficult:
When your dog knows what is expected when you say, "Lift your leg", you can tighten the leash more, so the leg has to be lifted higher. Also there will be occasions when the dog has to lift first one leg and then the other, to free the leash (see picture).

Special observations:
Should your dog have any joint disorders, be aware and modify the training accordingly.

Get treats or toys
from upon something
There are some challenging problems to solve in putting a treat or a toy upon something that seems impossible to climb from one angle, like a sloping rock. The dog has to use its brain to find out where to go, to get up on it and get the reward.

What it looks like:
The dog runs to and fro a couple of times, focused on the reward, and then tries to get around the rock, or in the case of a table, jumps up into the chair, and gets the treat or toy.

Step-by-step:
Start with putting the reward upon easy objects, so the dog learns to trust you that there is a solution. Place a reward on the top of a rock that is big enough that your dog cannot reach straight up from where it is. At the other side of that rock there must be an easier access so the dog can climb it and get the reward. Indoors, you can put a reward on a table or something as high as that. Place a chair beside the table for the dog to jump up on, in order to get the reward.

Make it more difficult:
Find more objects like these to let the dog work on.

Special observations:
If your dog has any joint problems it should not climb or jump.

Get the treats or toys
from under something
There are so many things you could put treats or toys under, for the dog to try and find and get hold of. Things could be hidden under, for example, a frisbee, a towel, a cup, a saucepan, a heap of toys, under a heap of laundry or under the corner of a carpet.

What it looks like:
You hide a treat or an attractive toy under something and entice the dog to find out how to get it.

When retrieving the favourite toy from a tree, it sometimes has to stretch a bit. Photo: Lehari

Which cup is hiding the treat? Photo: Prawitz

Step-by-step:

Always start with an easy exercise, such as hiding a treat under a paper cup, so the dog learns that there is a solution to every problem you present.

Make it more difficult:

There is a gradually increasing challenge depending on how you choose the obstacles the dog has to overcome to get the treat or toy.

Special observations:

Never give the dog a problem that is too difficult for it to solve. Always use an attractive treat or toy, so the dog will stay motivated and not give up.

Open paper boxes

Many things you buy come in paper boxes and paper bags, so you should have no problem finding them. Also save the empty rolls from kitchen and toilet papers — they are excellent because of the stiffer material. Do not worry about the cleaning up — ask the dog to do that (see "Clean up", on page 58).

What it looks like:

You put treats in one or several paper boxes and give them to your dog, as if it were Christmas.

Step-by-step:

This easy-to-do activation does not usually require any step-by-step development, other than if your dog is very small and has insufficient strength in the muscles of its mouth.

Make it more difficult:

You can put a box in another box and even yet another. Or you can hide several boxes and let the dog combine searching for them with opening them.

Special observations:

Normally dogs do not learn to open every box they see, as some dog-owners suspect. They just go for the ones that smell of the treat.

Pull the string

What it looks like:

At one end of a piece of string, under for example the sofa, there is a treat. The string sticks out and the dog grabs that end and pulls the treat out.

Step-by-step:

Begin with a small paper box tied to the end of the string that sticks out from under the sofa, and have a very attractive treat in another paper box tied to the other end, out of reach of the dog. Let it find out how to do this for itself. When it gets frustrated enough, it will grab the paper box and pull. Some dogs pull the string with their paws — any way is good.

Make it more difficult:

Put the treat on a door handle, upon a door, under a window — or wherever, and let the dog pull the string. Do not tie a paper box at the end of the string which it is supposed to pull.

Special observations:

If the treat is placed high up and the string hangs down, the dog might be scared when the treat falls, so start with smaller heights and gradually put the treat higher.

Laundry ball; tennis ball;
"Buster Cube"

Many plastic laundry balls, of the type intended to dispense soap powder inside the washing machine, are perfect toys to put small treats inside. When the dog rolls it about, treats are released through the holes. You can also make three or four holes in a tennis ball, or even better, a big-

ger plastic ball. There is also a special dog toy, "The Buster Cube", manufactured for mental activation of dogs, that most pet shops carry, and which works in a similar way.

What it looks like:
Your dog rolls and bounces around the ball until it is empty. This could take five to ten

The ball filled with treats will be rolled around until it is empty. Photo: Lehari

minutes, and tires the dog as much as a half-hour walk would do!

Step-by-step:
Either have very small treats or bigger holes when introducing this. The Buster Cube has two settings, "easy" and "difficult."

Make it more difficult:
When your dog has learned how to manipulate this toy, have bigger treats hidden or, if you are using a tennis or plastic ball, make a new ball with smaller holes.

Special observations:
The first time the dog plays with this type of toy, it should be very easy for it to get a treat out of it. Sometimes one has to throw a couple of treats to where the ball is, so the dog believes that they came from the toy.

Open lid
What it looks like:
When you give the dog a box (preferably a wooden one) with a lid, it will open it to get a toy or a treat.

Step-by-step:
Try to find a box that is to become a part of the dog's activation material, with a lid, attached by hinges at one end. At first let the lid be open and put a toy or a treat in the box. Ask the dog to get the reward. Next step is to have the lid a little bit open by putting something like a stick between the box and the lid. See to it, though, that the stick holds steady. Ask the dog again to get the reward. In the next step, have the lid shut, so the dog has to open the box with its nose to get the reward. Be there to give a little help if your dog seems like giving up.

Make it more difficult:
When the dog is good at opening the box, ask it to open it, but without any treat or toy inside. When the box is opened, you reward the dog from your hand. You could also turn the box upside down, the lid against the floor. Try to find some other boxes to do this exercise with. Try also a small plastic vitamin box with a hinged lid.

Special observations:
To get the lid to stay a little open, in the first few trials you may have to do some construction. Be sure it is steady, though, so the dog does not get scared if it shuts.

Get treats from
plastic boxes and bottles
Most plastic boxes and bottles have smaller openings than they are wide, and to get treats out of them require some skills and technique.

What it looks like:
You put some small treats in, for example, an empty and cleaned plastic ketchup bottle and give it to the dog, who manipulates it, rolls it and shakes it, until it is empty.

The dog needs to lift the basket in order to reach the toy. Photos: Lehari

You can hide treats in this cone that the dog has to try and reach. Photo: Prawitz

Step-by-step:
Start with an empty vitamin box or something that is easy to knock around and get the treats from, and let the dog solve the problem itself.

Make it more difficult:
Find boxes and bottles that have smaller openings. Hide them and let the dog find them first.

Special observations:
Take care the first time so that the dog does not give up. Also ensure that it does not chew on the plastic.

Nose work

The dog's sense of smell is its best sense, one that is overwhelmingly superior to that of man. Dogs live by the smells surrounding them, just as we live by looking at and listening to the scenery surrounding us. Dogs have a strong need to use this sense every day and all the time, exploring and defining what is happening around them. To let the dog use this faculty in cooperative efforts together with you, is to really give your dog moments of quality. Here are some suggestions of how to do it.

Find treats indoors
What it looks like:
Your dog searches in one or several rooms, finding treats you have hidden in different places, while you go about your own business.

Step-by-step:
Start with hiding a few small treats on the floor, some of which the dog can see, others behind the legs of chairs and tables. Gradually put the treats in places like cupboard handles and seats of chairs, wherever you can find a good spot. It will take the dog five to ten minutes to find 30 treats, and it will take you 20 seconds to hide them! You can do this as often as you want to.

Make it more difficult:
Find really difficult spots to hide the treats. Combine with problem-solving, like pulling a piece of string to get the treat, or lifting a lid to get to it.

Special observations:
The treats you hide should be as small as possible, to keep the dog motivated and prevent it becoming fat. Should there be any risk that your dog gets too many treats and you have concerns about its waistline, just cut down on the portions of its regular food a little bit. The risk, though, is very small, because the dog is using up most of the calories while working.

Find treats in the yard
What it looks like:
Your dog searches for treats in the yard, while you go about your own business.

Step-by-step:
Let the dog see when you throw small pieces of treats, like dry dog food or corn flakes, out on the grass. Tell it to find them. After a couple of times, or now and again, you can really hide the treats, on and under objects, stuck into the bark of a tree, upon leaves — you will find many different spots when you start this. If you are pressed for time, take a handful of corn flakes, if the dog likes that, throw it up in the air and let the wind spread it around. It takes you a few seconds and may keep our dog occupied with quality time for at least ten minutes, making it as tired as if you had been walking for 30 minutes.

Make it more difficult:
Find really difficult spots in which to hide the treats. Combine with problem-solving,

These treats are hidden in the bag. Photo: Prawitz

like pulling a piece of string to get the treat or lift a lid to get to it.

Special observations:

The treats you hide should be as small as possible, to keep the dog motivated and avoid it becoming fat.

Should there be any risk that your dog gets too many treats and you have concerns about its waistline, just cut down on the portions of its regular food a little bit. The risk, though, is very small, because the dog is using up most of the calories while working.

Find the keys

What it looks like:

When you ask your dog to "Find my keys", it starts to search for them and, when they are found, it will sit down. One day you may be thankful for teaching this to the dog — ask me, I know!

Step-by-step:

Start by putting your keys on the ground, preferably in some grass, so the dog cannot see them too easily. Place an attractive small treat upon the keys. Bring the dog, which should be on the leash, and sit it on your left side, three feet in front of the keys. Wait a second so you can see that the dog is calm and focused. Should that not be the case, perhaps it needs a walk before training.

Hold the leash short in your left hand and make a sweeping gesture with your right

down to the ground and against the keys, as you say "Find my keys!" Let the dog immediately walk in the direction of your hand, nose to the ground. When it finds the treat and eats it, praise and hold up the keys in front of the dog's nose. Repeat the same exercise a couple of times and then take a long break.

After the break, do the exercise again one time exactly as before. After that comes the next step. Place the treat on the ground and the keys on top, so the dog has to put them aside to take its treat. Repeat a few times, but start to change location just a few feet away from the last exercise. This is to ensure that the dog does not get conditioned to just one location.

After a long break — for example, the next day — go back one step in the development of the exercises, so as to remind the dog of the task. Then start to increase the distance for it to search, but carefully, not too big steps at a time.

When you have done these exercises about fifteen to twenty times in slightly different places, and with breaks in between, place the keys in the grass, but no treat. Hide the treat in your left hand, give the sign, a sweeping gesture, with your right hand, and ask the dog to find the keys. When it smells the keys you will see an increase of interest, and in the very second the nose touches the keys, praise and give the treat. Repeat several times, but with breaks interspersed. Maintain the skill by having the dog find your keys now and again.

Dogs can learn to detect personal items such as keys, purses or similar. Photo: Lehari

Make it more difficult:

Teach the dog to search in successively larger areas. Teach the dog to bring the keys to you. Teach it to find other people's keys too. You do not have to go through the exercises from the beginning when training with different keys, because the dog will easily generalize the smell of metal.

Special observations:
None.

Trailing
What it looks like:
You and your dog follow a trail that you half an hour or so earlier have walked, leaving your scent and some rewards on the way. The right word to say when you start is "Seek."

Step-by-step:
To begin with, you and your dog must find a spot where there are no people and no fresh trails of people or dogs, a kind of a private place if you can find one. You tie the dog up, show a toy and get it eager to have it. Then you walk away out of sight for 25 plus yards, straight out, and hide the toy. Go back, wait for a minute and let the dog pick up your trail, leading to the toy. When it finds it, play for a moment to reinforce the performance.

Do the same thing a couple of times, but walk in other directions and that's all for one day. In subsequent training sessions, gradually add some yards to the trail and also add some angles, making right and left turns. Also, as the trail becomes longer, say 50 yards, add some more toys. Try to put one toy every 25–30 yards, as long as the dog is a beginner with this exercise.

Make it more difficult:
Making trailing more difficult comes naturally, when you pick more rough terrain to walk in and when you prolong the trail, and when your dog has to work longer before it finds the reward. Wait gradually longer, but not much more than one hour, before you let the dog start trailing. This exercise will also be more difficult when it is windy and when other people have walked on the grounds. Trailing other people is a good way to develop this further still.

Special observations:
Many times, the scent is not exactly where your footsteps were, but a little bit on the side, due to the wind, so let your dog decide where to sniff and correct only if it goes too far away from the actual trail. If you like this kind of training, join a dog club where you will get professional guidance.

Follow a scent trail indoors
What it looks like:
This is something to do before you intend to wash the floor. For example with a piece

The dog follows the trail that was laid out by a person.
Photo: Lehari

of a dried sausage, make a trail indoors, leading to that treat, and your dog will eagerly pick up the scent and find the reward.

Step-by-step:
Have your dog in another room while you make the scent trail on the floor from one starting point and around the corner of some piece of furniture in the same room. Bring the dog and make it sit at the start line and concentrate for a few seconds. Then you point at the trail, saying "Look for it", or "Find", or something like that. Do not use the same word as in outdoors trailing after a person. Gradually prolong the distance.

Make it more difficult:
Not putting any pressure on the treat when you hold it to the floor will make it leave a weaker scent. When your dog is good at this, you could tie a piece of string and just pull the treat over the floor. Also wait longer and longer before you start the dog, but not too long.

Special observations:
Do not do this more than one time in one room, because if there are scent trails from the earlier treat that are too close, the dog might be confused.

Search for people
What it looks like:
The dog runs in a zigzag way in an open area, trying to pick up a scent from a person in the wind, and finally finds that person hidden behind some bushes or some such place. You need a family member or a friend to play the role of the "lost person".

Step-by-step:
Without the dog knowing, let the "lost person" hide 25–30 yards from the starting point you have chosen. This person must not leave a trail from that point, but instead walk around in a big semi-circle to the finish point and hide, holding a few treats or an attractive toy. You should be positioned downwind from the "lost person".

Wait two or three minutes, then go to the starting point with your dog. Just stand there and say nothing, but be observant. When you see that your dog is picking something up in the wind, let it loose as you command "Search!" The dog will do the rest. Repeat the exercise, but in somewhat different places, just a couple of times. When your dog seems to know what this is about, gradually increase the distance to the "lost person", up to around 100 yards.

Make it more difficult:
The rougher the terrain and the more trees there are, the more difficult the exercise will be more.

Special observations:
Depending on wind and other conditions, your dog may run to or away from places where you believe there could be any scent. Do not try to control it; rather let it work on its own as much as possible. Only if it runs

away in the opposite direction, seemingly not interested, should you call it back. If you like this kind of training, join a dog club where you will get professional guidance.

Point at special objects
What it looks like:
You ask the dog to point with its nose at something you have selected out of different objects when you say "Find." When this exercise is completed you can have a lot of fun with it. For example when you have guests and you ask your dog to show you a book in the shelf, or a special cabinet door, or where the remote control to the VCR is, etc.

Step-by-step:
This is a discrimination exercise, where the dog is taught to distinguish between objects that might look the same, but only one of which has your scent on it. Start with two pieces of narrow-section timber, four inches long. When you get them, for example from a timber yard or a hardware store, get several pieces, because you are soon going to advance this exercise.

Be sure not to touch any of the pieces. Preferably handle them with a pair of tongs, or at least wear gloves. Keep them outdoors so the wind will erase any smells from them.

Before you start the exercise, mark one piece with an X on both short sides. This is the one the dog is going to point at. Hold this in your hand with a firm grip for a few seconds, so your smell really gets on to it. Put it on the floor or on the ground, place a small treat under it and, with a pair of tongs (or wearing a glove), place the other piece of wood a couple inches away from it. Get the dog and have it sit next to you, three feet from the objects.

Make a sweeping gesture down to the ground and against the objects, as you say "Find." Let the dog immediately walk in the direction of your hand, nose low. When it finds the treat and eats it, praise and hold up the piece of wood in front of the dog's nose. Repeat the same exercise a couple of times and then take a long break. Repeat again, but in a couple of different places.

The next step is to let the dog find the right piece of wood, but with no treat under it. You praise and give the treat when your dog's nose is close to the right object.

When this is going well, add one more piece of wood, again handling it with tongs or gloves, and repeat the same exercise as above. Later you can add more and more pieces in the same manner.

When the dog is good at this, do the same, but with other objects, like pieces of metal or plastic. When you are out for a walk you can touch a pinecone or a stick, and place it among other pinecones or sticks, for the dog to find.

Make it more difficult:
Handle one book from the shelf so it gets your scent, especially on the back of the

The dog chooses between four different items. Photo: Prawitz

cover, without touching any of the others, and replace it. Place yourself and your dog about two feet away and ask it to "Find", while making the sweeping gesture towards the books. Be observant, and when your dog sniffs at the right book, praise immediately and reward with a treat. Repeat this until the dog has learned. Later, try other objects and leave progressively less scent, so you finally just touch the object with a finger.

Combine this exercise with "fetch", so the dog brings you the object you ask for.

Another version of the exercise: the dog only receives a treat if he touches the bell with his nose. Photo: Prawitz

Special observations:
Do not force or overdo this, it is very tiresome.

Balance

In nature there are no paved ways; only rough terrain. And wolves, to be able to catch their prey, have to move faster than it, as the prey flees into the bushes, over and under fallen trees, uphill and downhill. So our dogs have inherited the ability to find their way across all sorts of terrain, even in dark, in high-speed pursuit. Not only that, they have an actual need for the kind of challenge provided in overcoming different obstacles. This enhances their self-esteem, makes them more secure out on walks and provides a good work-out for different muscles. Here follow some suggestions that you could try out, but you should also try to find exercises of your own that work with your dog.

Agility

The masterpiece of balance exercises is of course the sport of agility, where dogs train and compete on an obstacle course. This has been shown to give frightened dogs courage, insecure dogs self-esteem, shy dogs go-ahead spirit, and passive dogs a good quality of life. And it does not matter if you have a miniature dog or a giant one. It is, though, not for every dog, exceptions being above all dogs with joint disorders. Your local dog club can provide you with more information on where to go to join an agility class.

Your own obstacle course
You can also build your own course in your garden quite easily. Just look at the pictures and you will find a lot of ideas and inspiration. See to it, though, that it is quite stable and not slippery, especially after rain.

What it looks like:
You walk beside your dog, enticing it with praise and treats to go up on a balance walk, jump up on a stump (or likewise), climbing on a ladder with big steps, encouraging it to jump a hurdle and zigzag through poles you have put in the ground.

Step-by-step:
Let your dog become properly acquainted with each obstacle before you make any changes to your course. Motivate with treats all the time—no force ever. Always warm up with a walk prior to letting your dog attempt any obstacles. Also massage the muscles before the work.

Make it more difficult:
You could raise the hurdles, make the ups and downs on the dog-walk more steep and increase the height of it, raise the ladder up from ground so it becomes more

If no suitable objects are available, a person can act as a substitute. Photos: Prawitz

Agility training is suited for all dogs without joint problems. Photo: Lehari

A bench can be used for various agility exercises.
Photo: Prawitz

Nature offers unlimited possibilities for agility exercises. Photo: Prawitz

like a dog-walk, train on stumps that are smaller and narrower, and so on. You start to send your dog to different obstacles, while standing still yourself.

Special observations:
Do not try to force the dog to attempt any obstacle: that will just frighten it and is counter-productive. If it falls or is hurt for some reason, do not comfort it, because a comforting voice, when the dog hears that you feel sorry for it, will reinforce its anxiety. Make it happy again by encouraging it to retry the obstacle immediately, and praise intensively and give a few extra treats.

If you are not sure of the condition of your dog's joints, take it to a veterinarian before you start with these exercises.

Nature— a big obstacle course
When you are out walking your dog in the countryside, there are almost unlimited possibilities for the dog to do some balance training. You will find fallen trees and rocks and steep uphill and downhill paths to work on. Just look around and you will discover all that nature has in store for your dog's balance exercises.

What it looks like:
You entice your dog to balance on fallen trees and jump up on stones and rocks, praising and rewarding with treats. Sometimes you ask it to sit, lie down, turn around, wave and other things, while on an obstacle.

Step-by-step:
Start with easy-to-manage obstacles and gradually move on to more difficult ones.

Make it more difficult:
Sending your dog ahead up on an obstacle, asking it to climb and balance on a small stone and finding more difficult ones as well as doing tricks on the obstacles.

Special observations:
Do not try to force the dog to attempt any obstacle. If it falls or is hurt for some reason, do not comfort it, because a comforting voice will reinforce the anxiety. Make the dog happy again by encouraging it to retry the obstacle immediately, then praise intensively and give a few extra treats. If you are not sure of the condition of your dog's joints, take it to a veterinarian before you start with these exercises.

On a walk in a park or
in the neighbourhood
There are often possibilities to find obstacles right around the corner. Look around and you will find them. There may be building materials, low walls, some small rocks and some things to jump over or on top of.

What it looks like:
You entice your dog to balance on walls, jump up on or over stones and obstacles, praising and rewarding with treats.

You can combine several exercises: the dog has to search, retrieve and crawl underneath an obstacle.
Photos: Prawitz

Step-by-step:
You start with easy-to-manage obstacles and gradually move on to more difficult ones.

Make it more difficult:
Sending your dog ahead up on an obstacle, asking it to climb and balance on a small stone and finding more difficult ones, doing tricks on the obstacles.

Special observations:
Do not try to force the dog to attempt any obstacle. If it falls or is hurt for some reason, do not comfort it, because a comforting voice will reinforce the anxiety. Make the dog happy again by encouraging it to retry the obstacle immediately, then praise intensively and give a few extra treats. If you are not sure of the condition of your dog's joints, take it to a veterinarian before you start with these exercises.

Use a special harness to let the dog carry your shopping or travel items. Photo: Prawitz

Miscellaneous

Let the dog come along

How easy it is just to leave the dog at home when you go for short errands. But stop there! It may not be such a great activation to sit in a car, but it is always something, and there could be opportunities for the dog to come out for an exchange of pee-mails in a park. It is not a good thing, however, if you have to leave your dog more than short moments in the car, especially on hot and sunny days. Dogs should not spend a lot of time in cars – that's never appropriate. A car is a means of transportation, not a means of detention.

If you are comfortable with taking your dog to the local shops—and if there is no risk of it being stolen when you tie it outside—let it come along. Buy a backpack or a small cart and your dog will proudly help you to carry home the hot dogs, the chickens and the dog food.

When you are going out to visit neighbours or friends, ask if your dog is welcome too, of course on the condition that it is well-behaved—which it will be, after just a few weeks of mental activation.

Bibliography

Fox, M. W. Understanding Your Dog.
New York: Coward, McCann & Geoghegan
Inc., 1974

Hall, R. and Sharp, H. (eds) Wolf and Man.
New York: Academic Press, 1978

Lopez, B.H. Vargen och Människan.
Stockholm: Liber förlag, 1978

Mech, D. The Wolf.
New York: Natural History Press, 1970

Mortensson, F. J. Animal Behaviour: Theory
and Research.
California: Brooks/Cole Publishing
Company, 1975

Peters, R. Dance of the Wolves.
New York: McGraw Hill Book Company,
1985

Seligman, M. E. P. Helplessness.
On Depression, Developement and Death.
San Francisco: Freeman, 1975

Trumler, E. Hunde ernst genommen.
Munich: R. Piper & Co Verlag, 1978

Whitney, L. F. Dog Psychology.
New York: Howell Bookhouse, 1971.

Zimen, E. The Wolf—a species in danger.
New York: Delacorte Press, 1981.